COFFEE THEMES AND FLOWER AR...

COFFEE IS my best FRIEND

MOTIVATIONAL

COLORING BOOK FOR ADULT
STRESS RELIEVING PATTERNS

Jupiter Coloring

Printed in U.S.A.

Copyright 2017

All right reserved. This Coloring books or any potion thereof many not be reproduced or used in any manner whatsoever without the exoress written permission of the publisher except.

This book belongs to:
_____

COLOR TEST PAGE

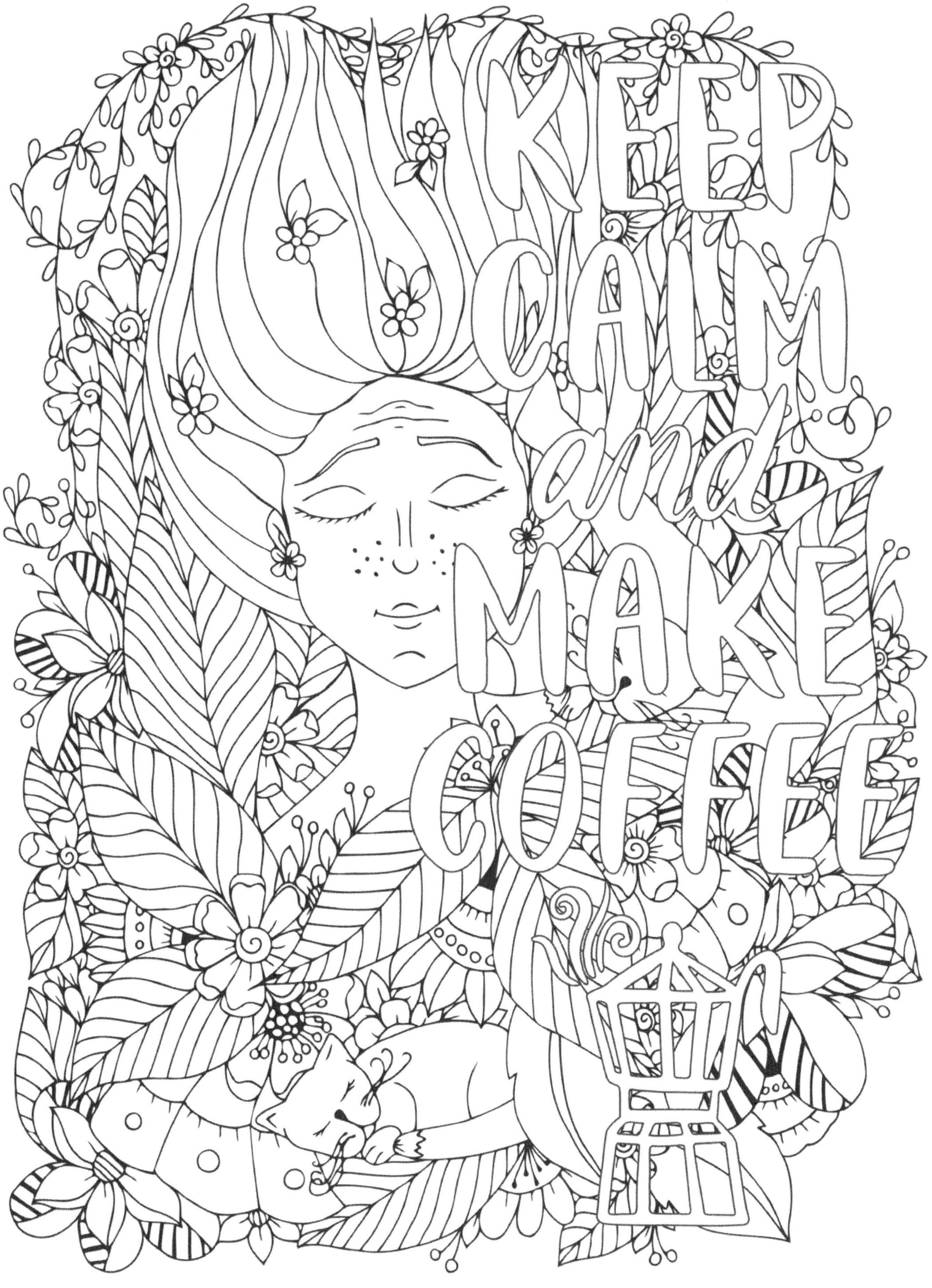
KEEP
CALM
and
MAKE
COFFEE

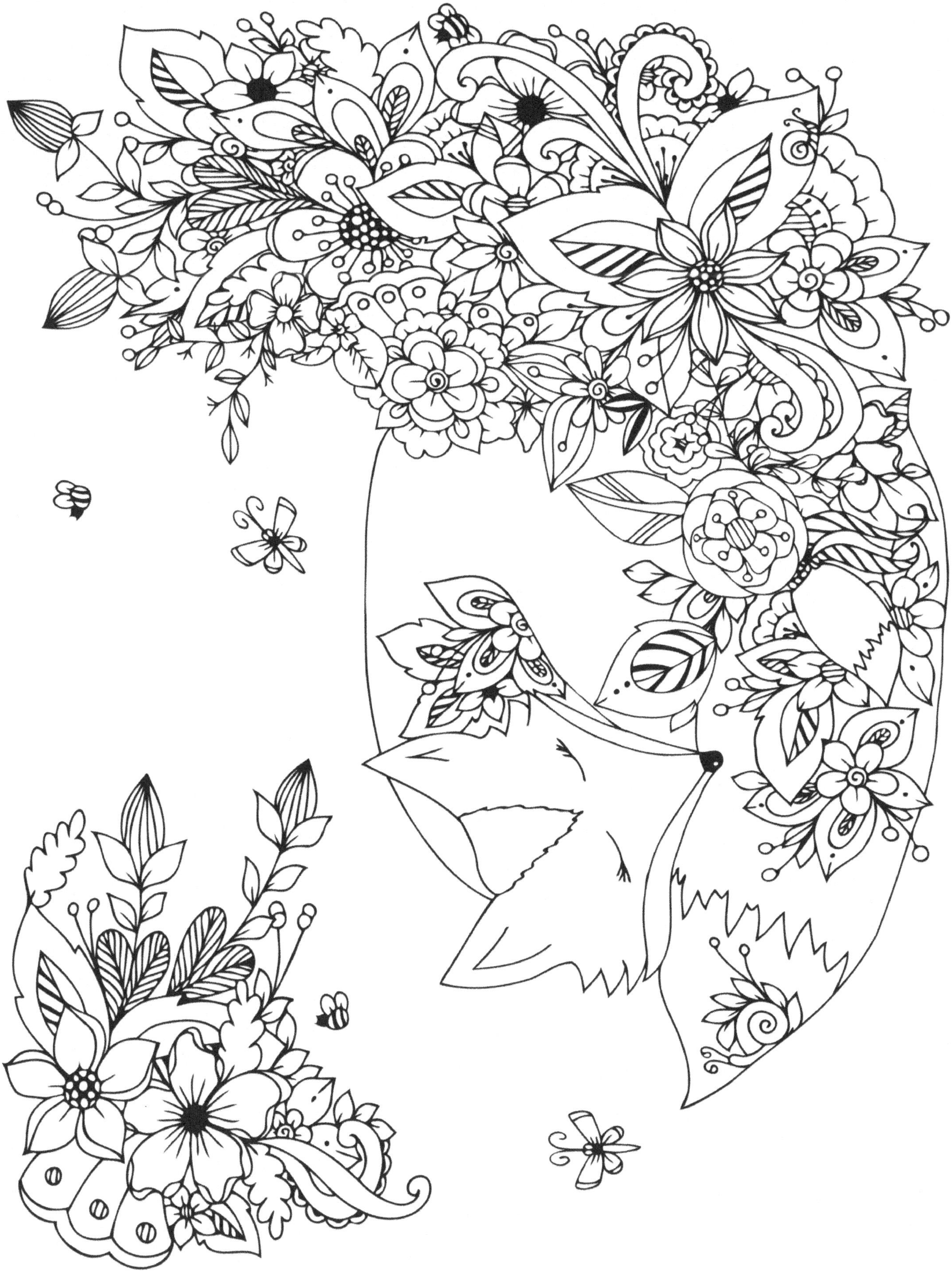

Life begins after coffee

DRINK GOOD Coffee READ GOOD Books

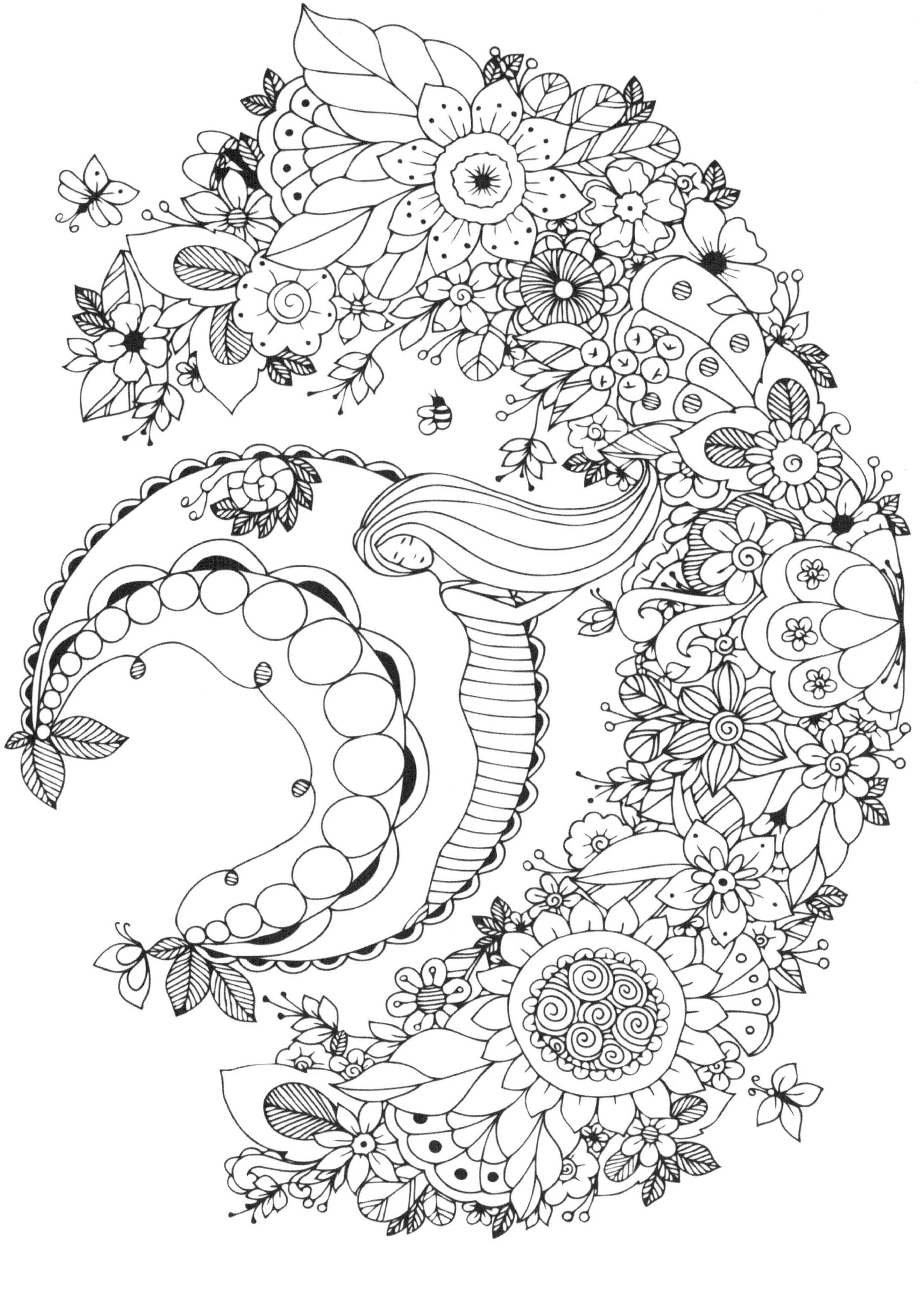

Be Amazing today, but first, COFFEE

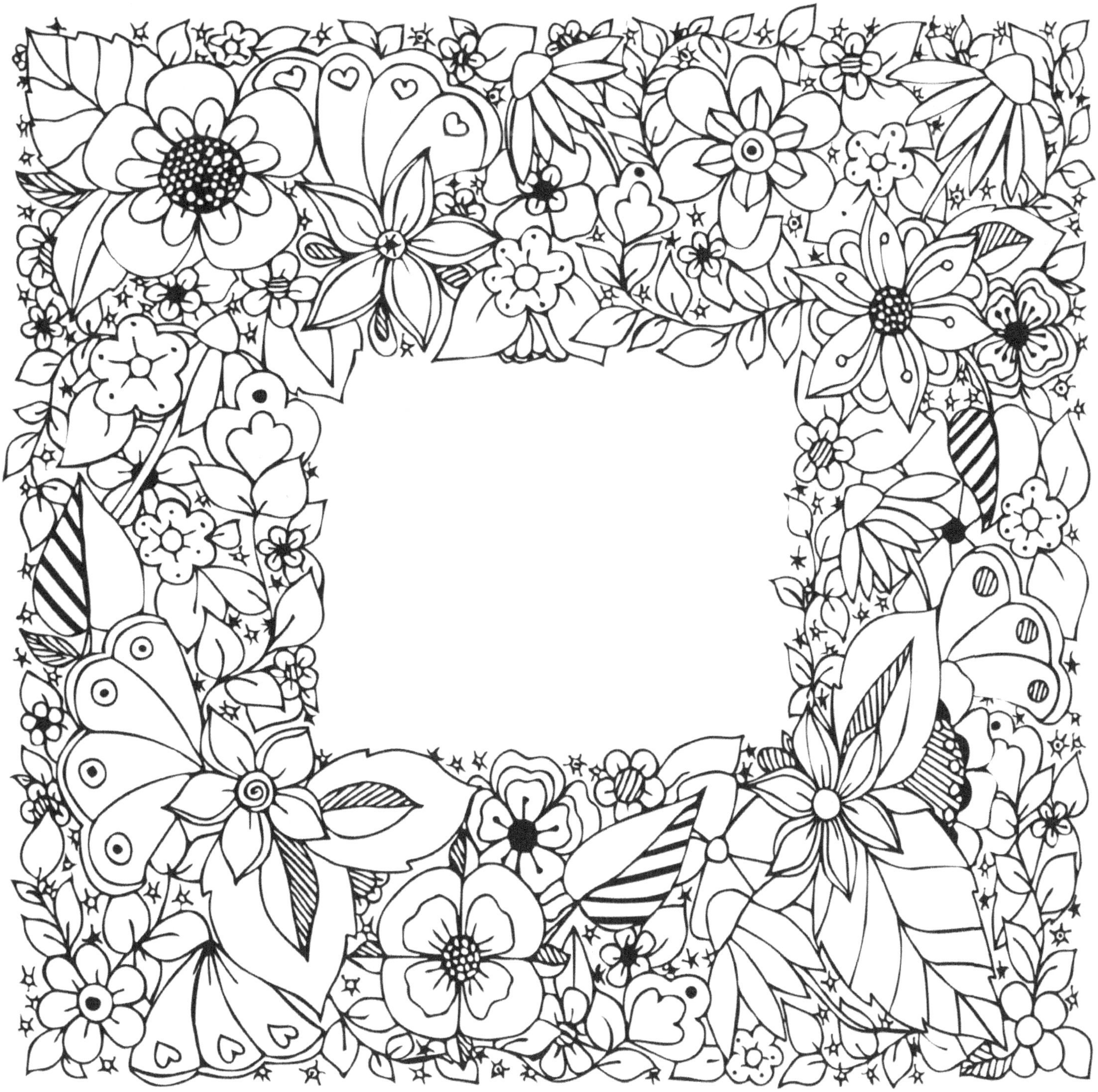

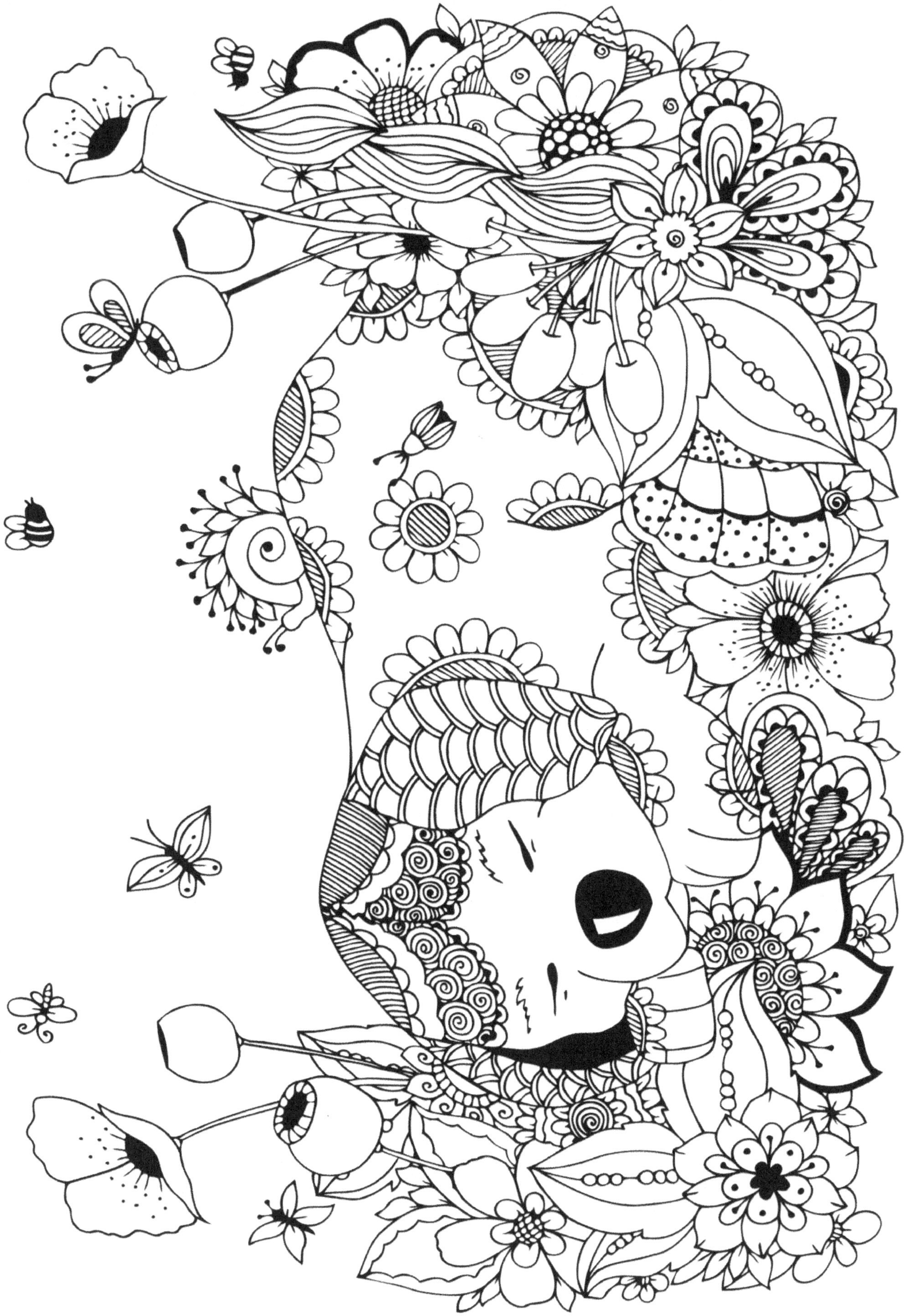

COFFEE doesn't ask silly questions COFFEE understands.

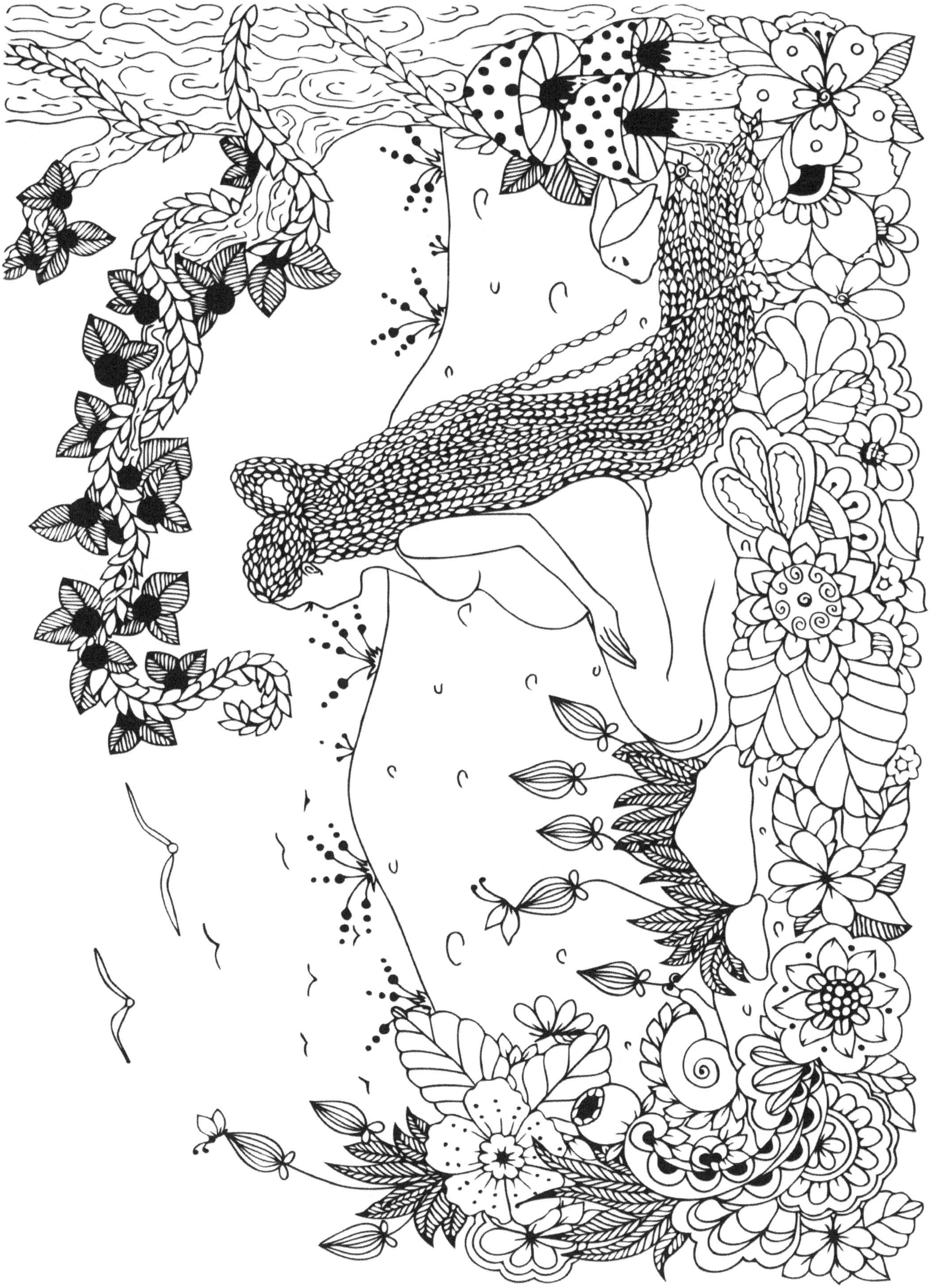

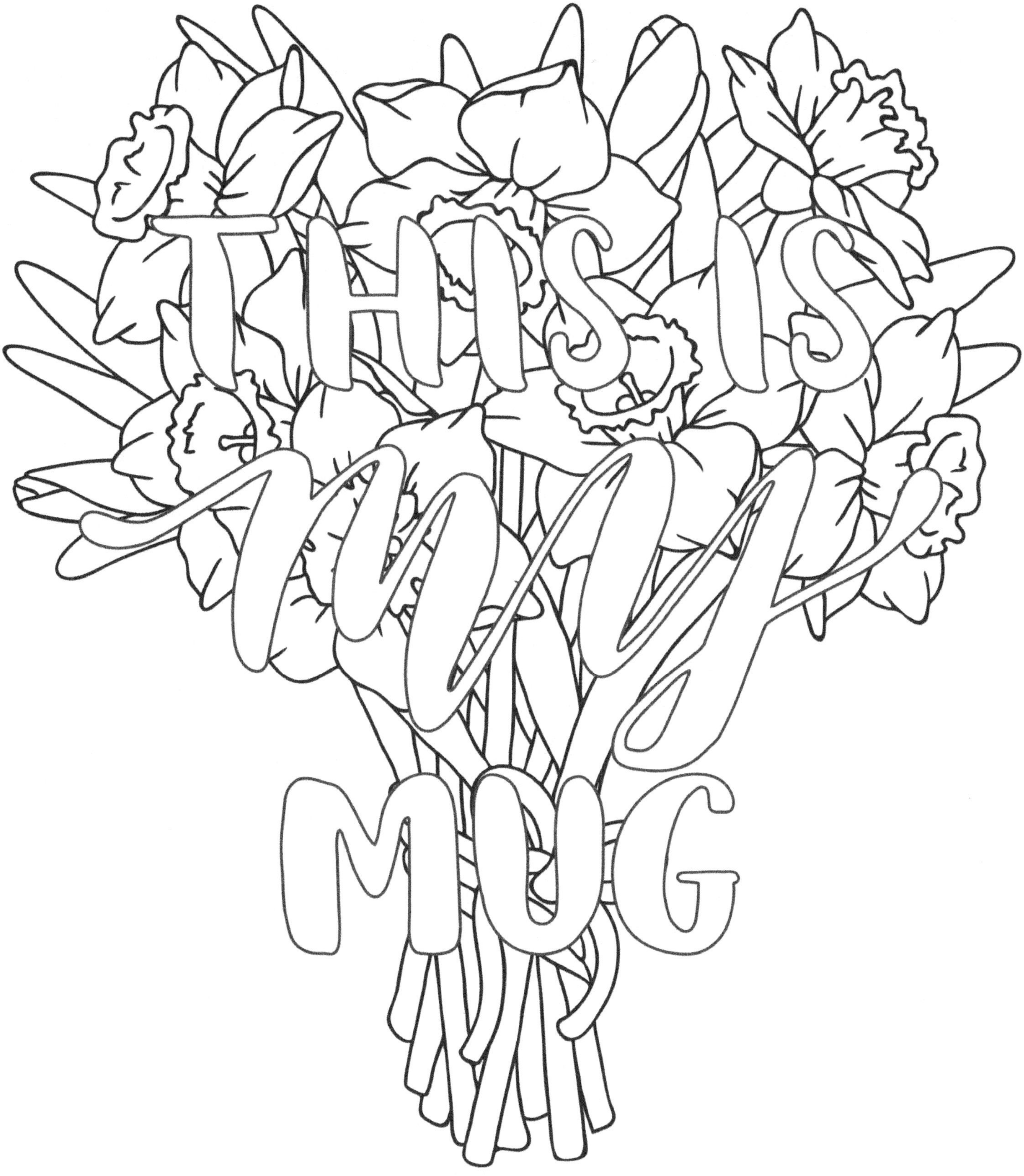
THIS IS
my
MUG

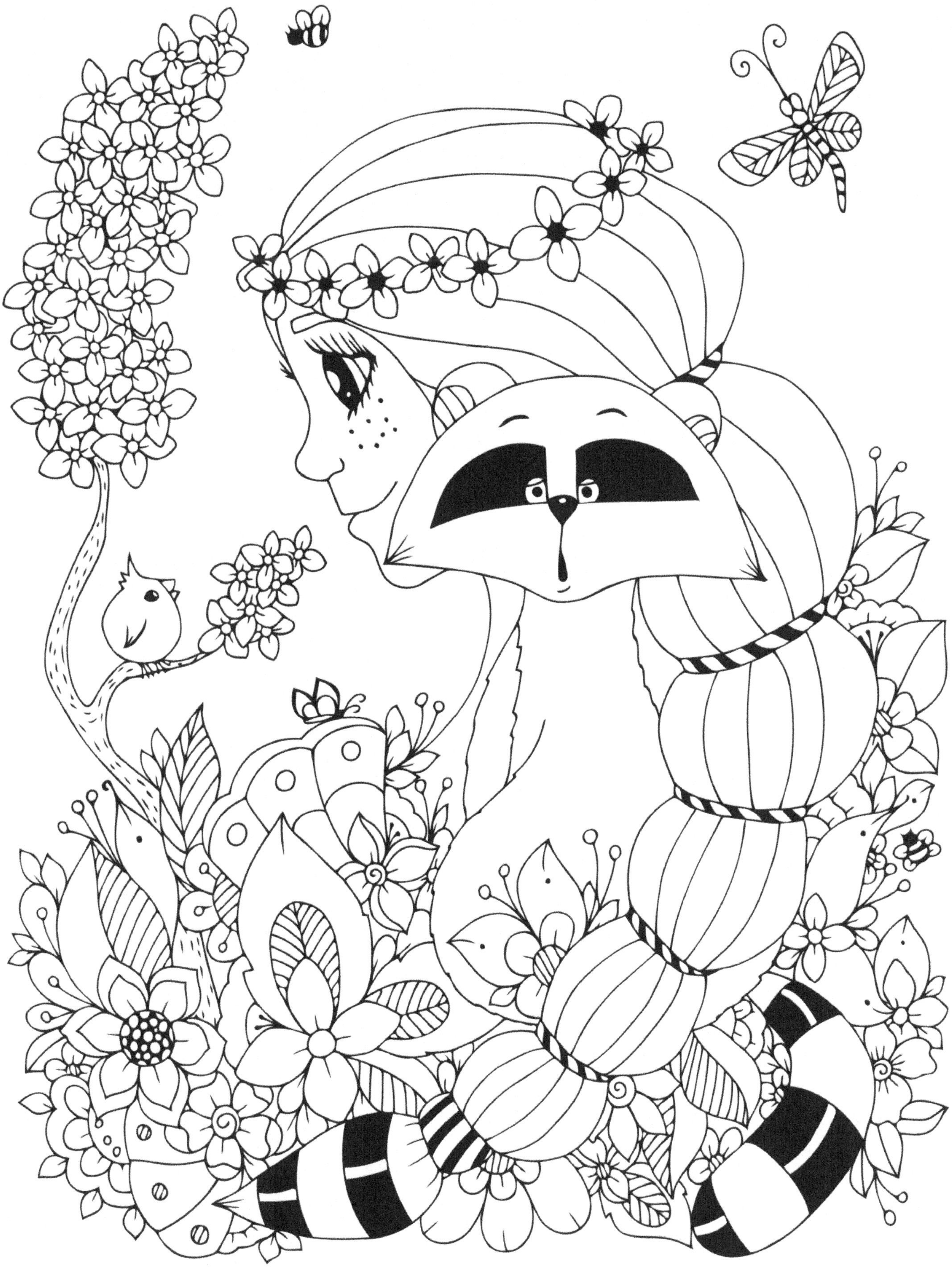

DRINK GOOD Coffee

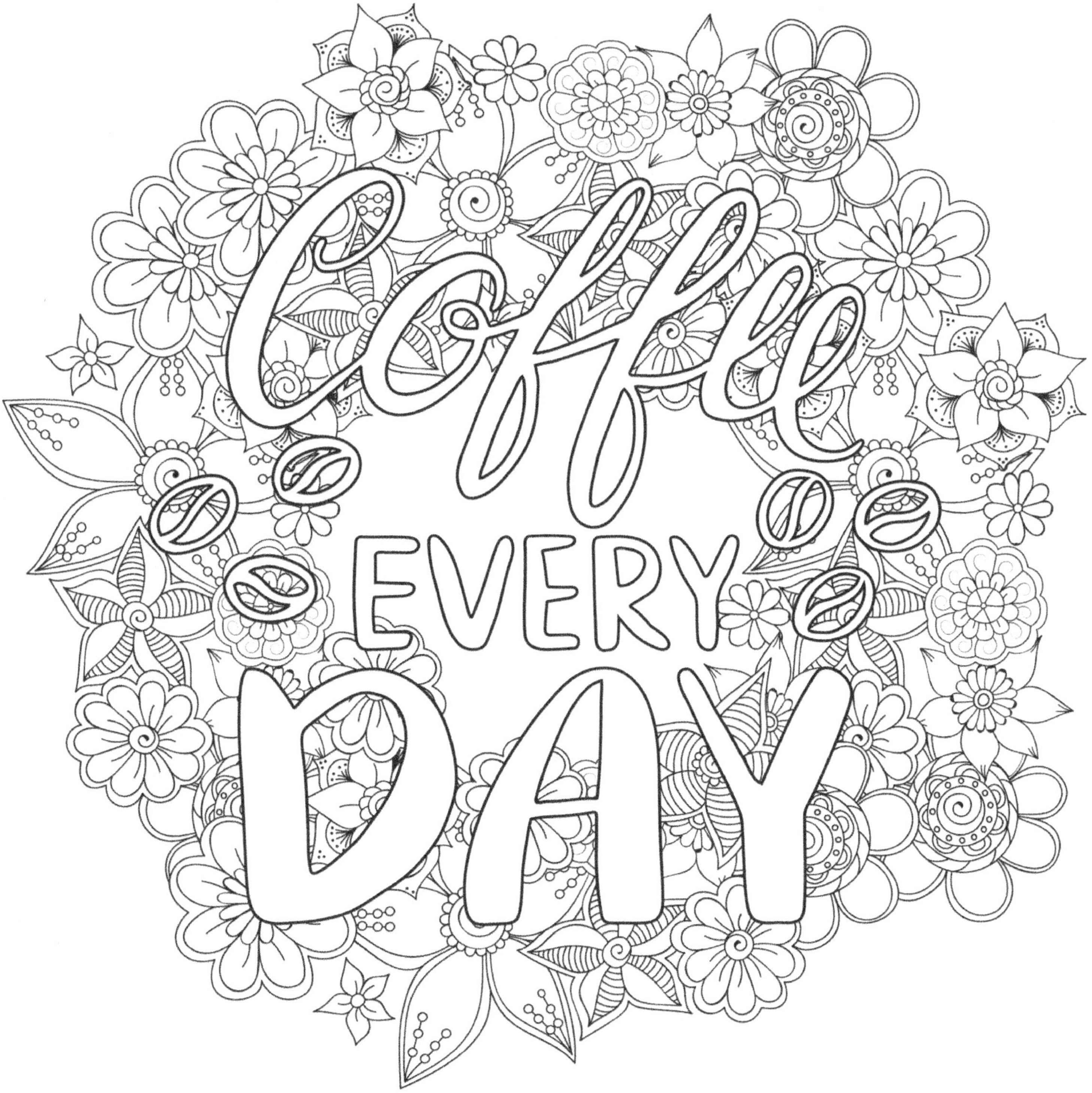
Coffee
EVERY
DAY

I love you more than COFFEE

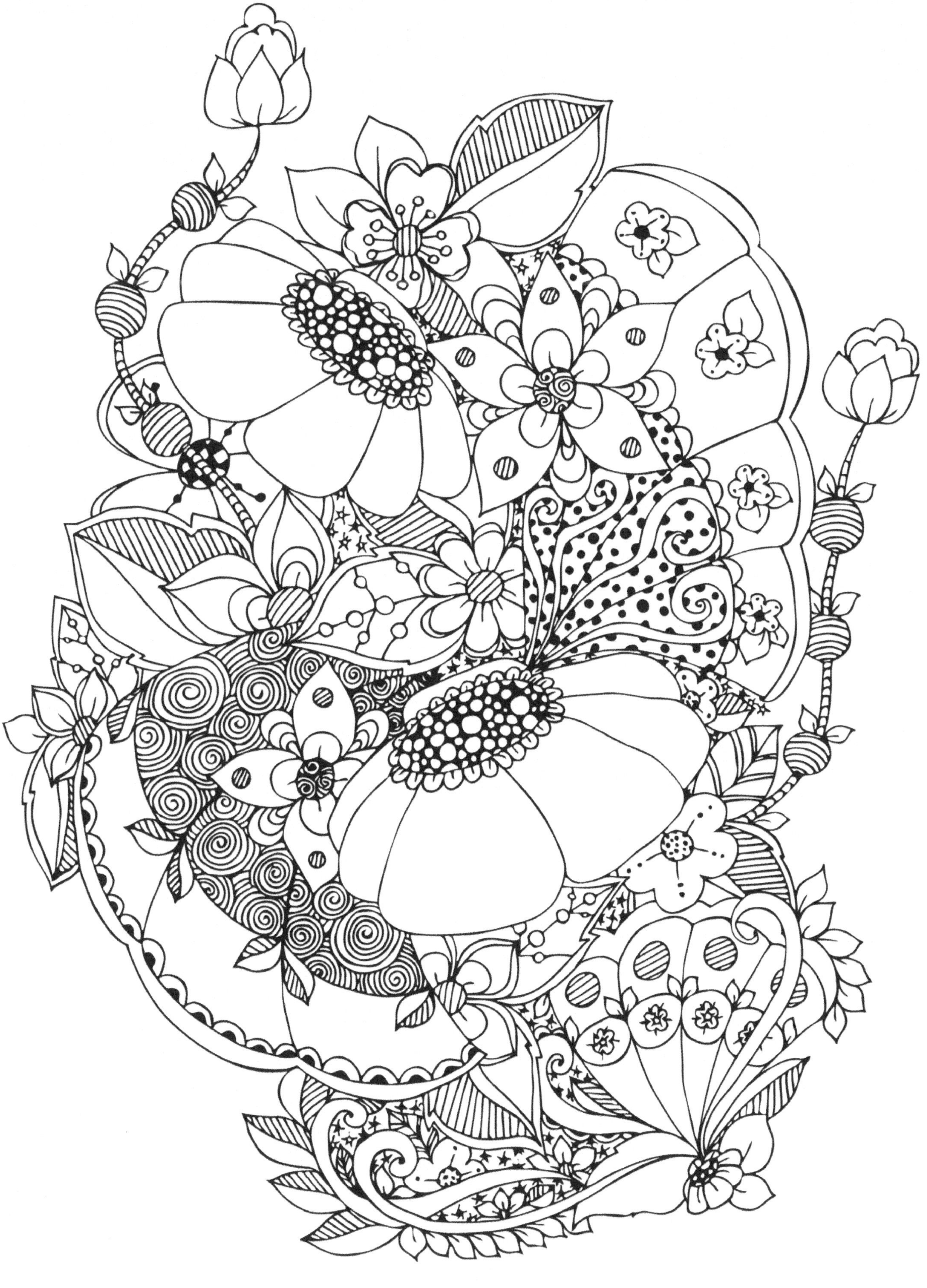

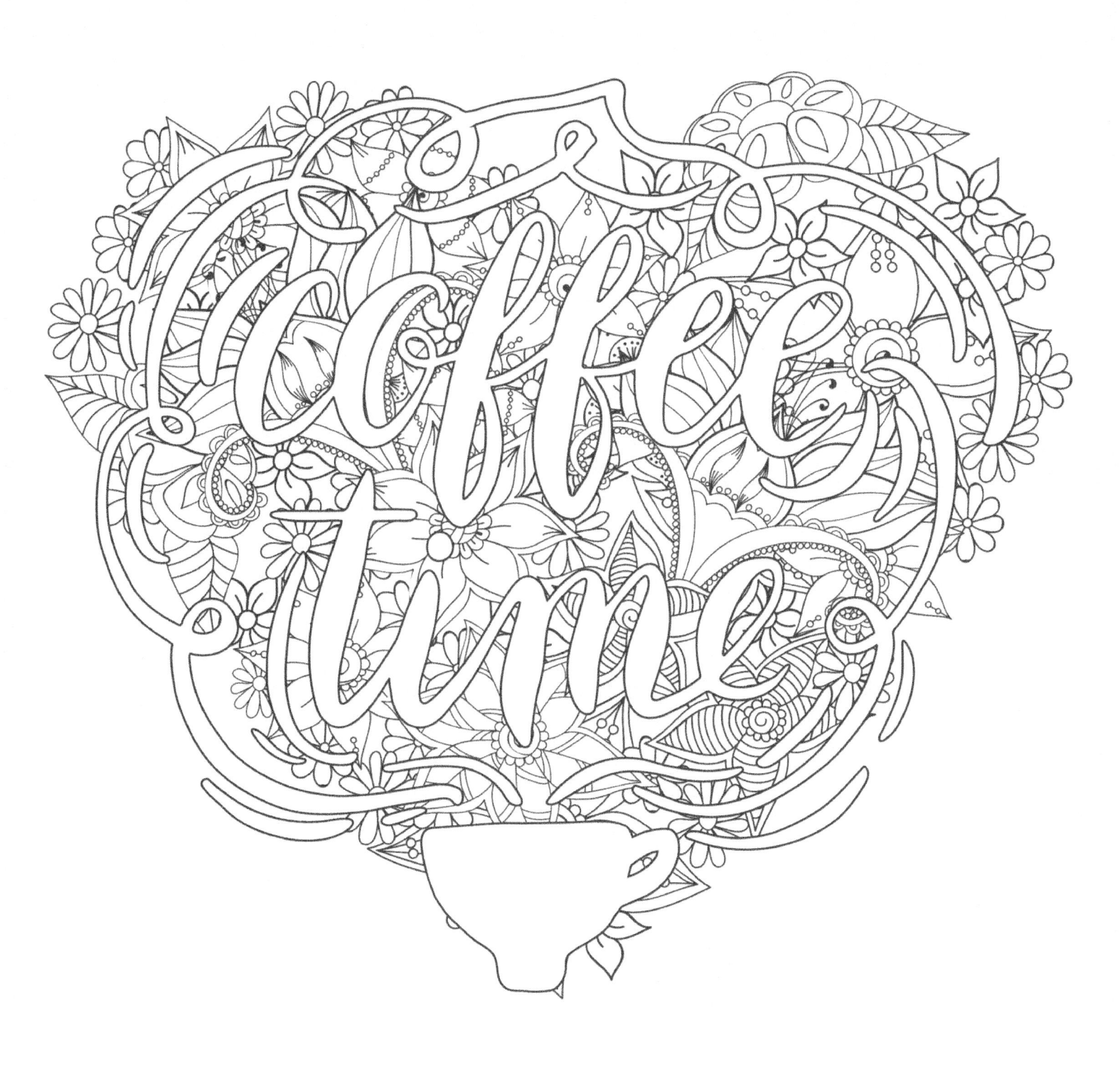
coffee
time

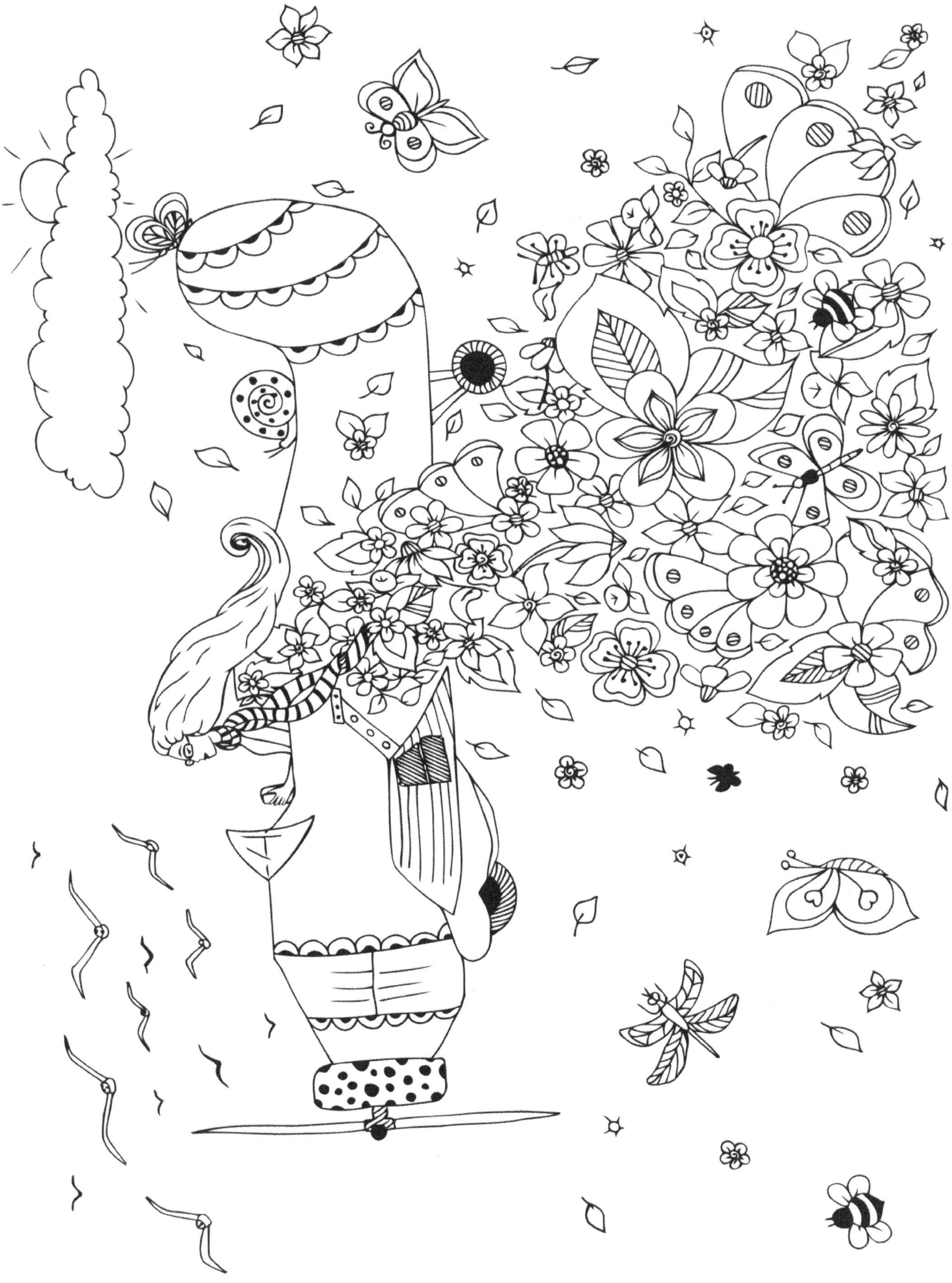

all you need is love and more coffee

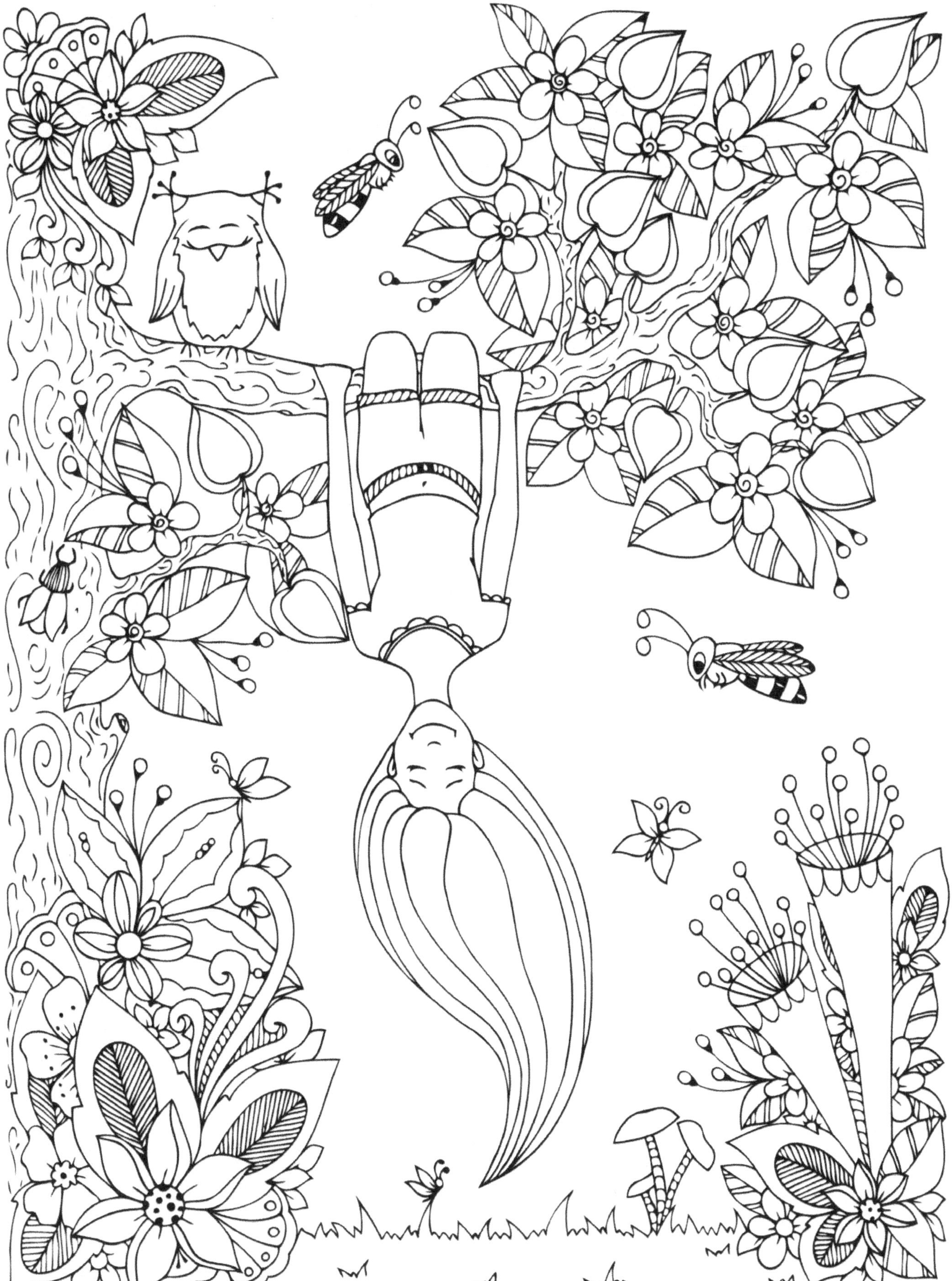

COFFEE IS ALWAYS a good IDEA

KEEP CALM and MAKE COFFEE

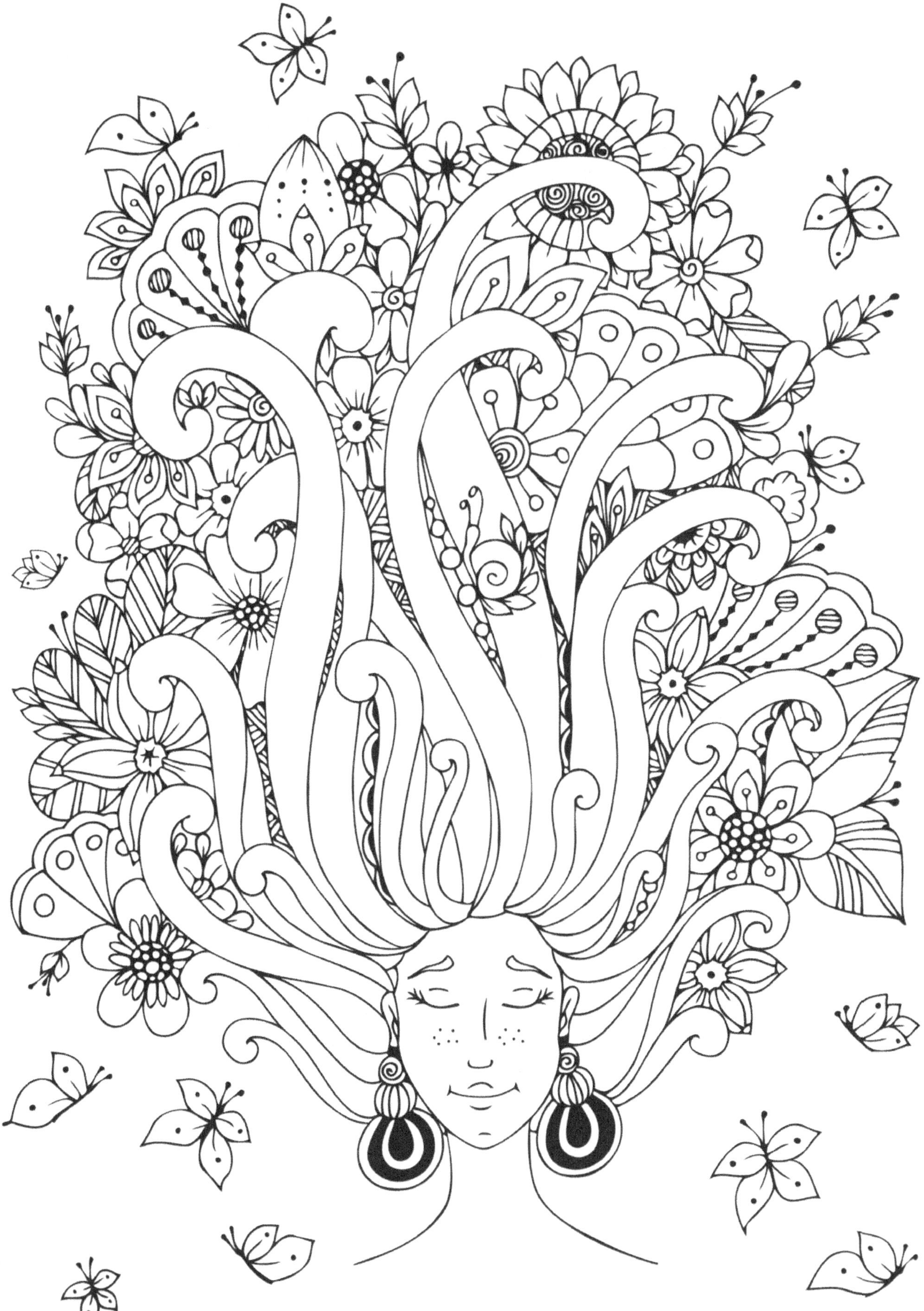

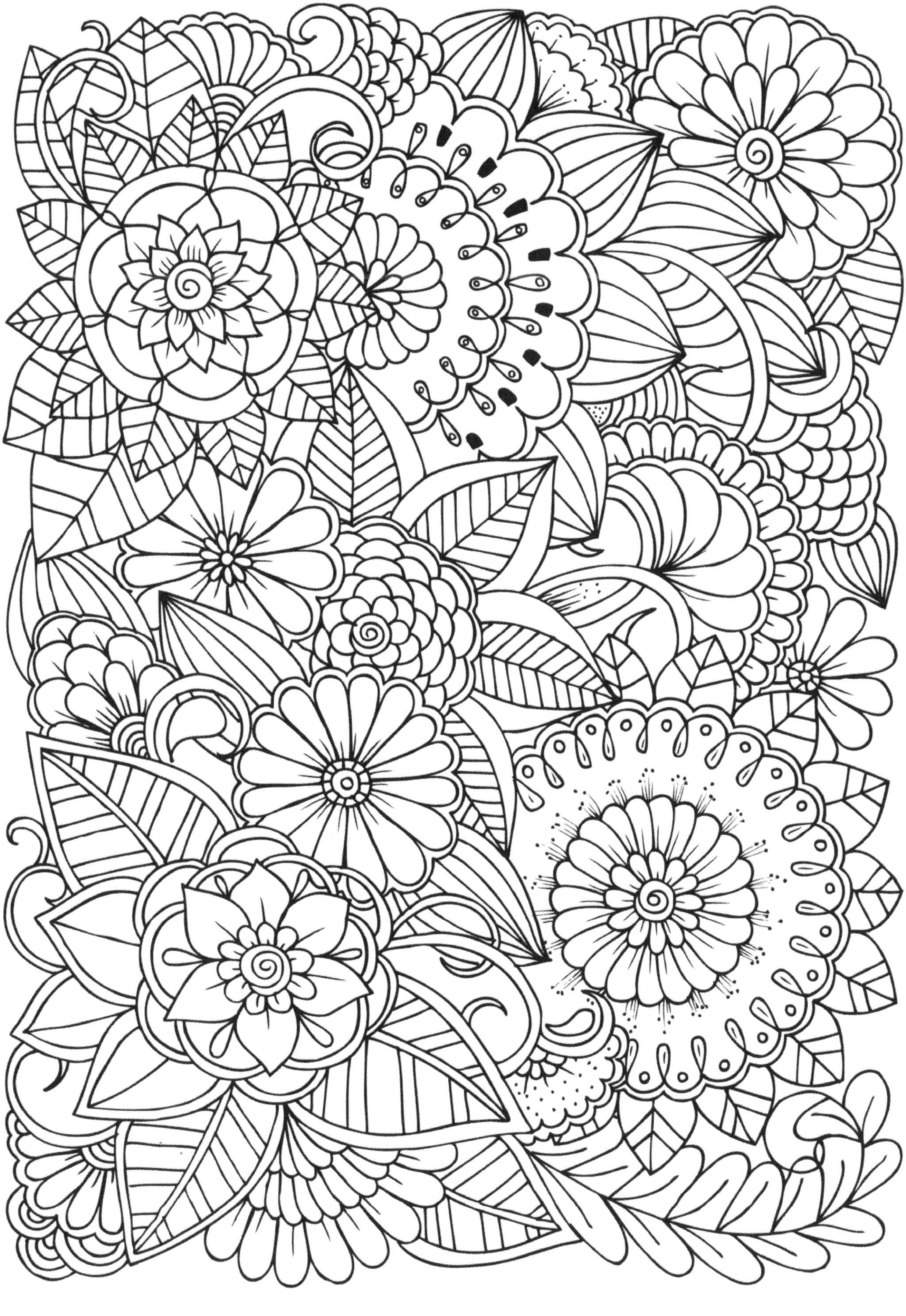

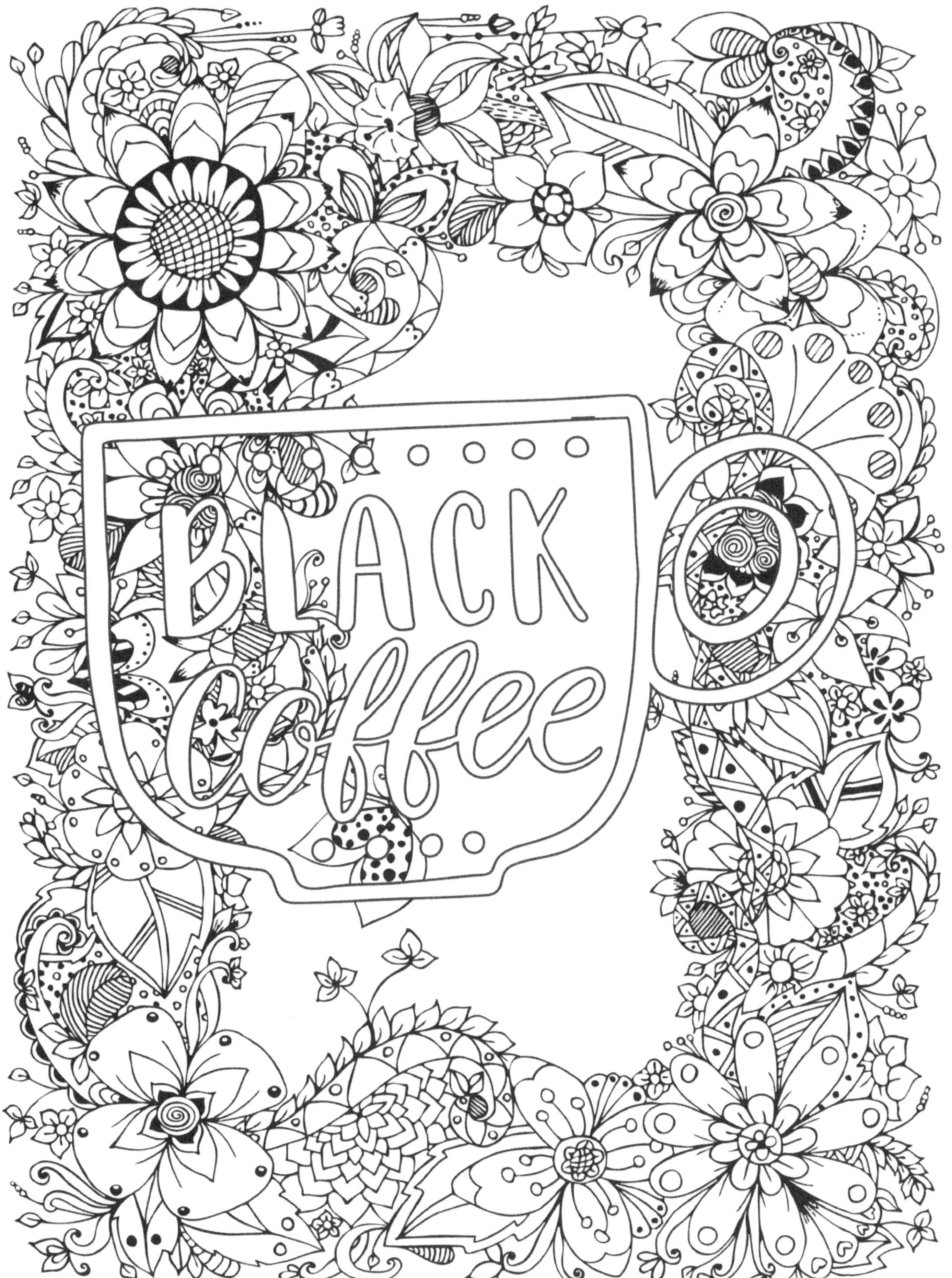
BLACK
coffee

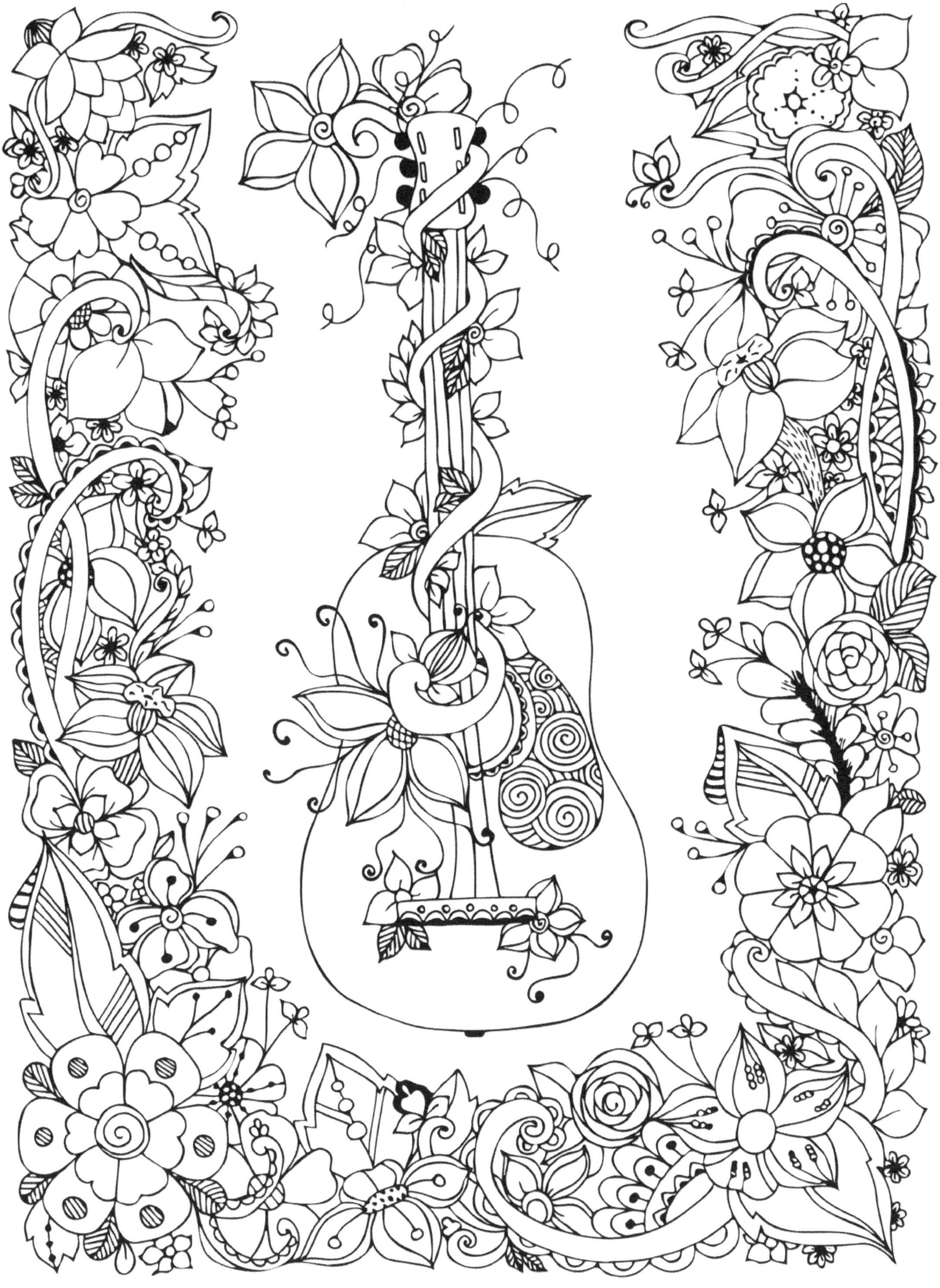

Coffee tea anything

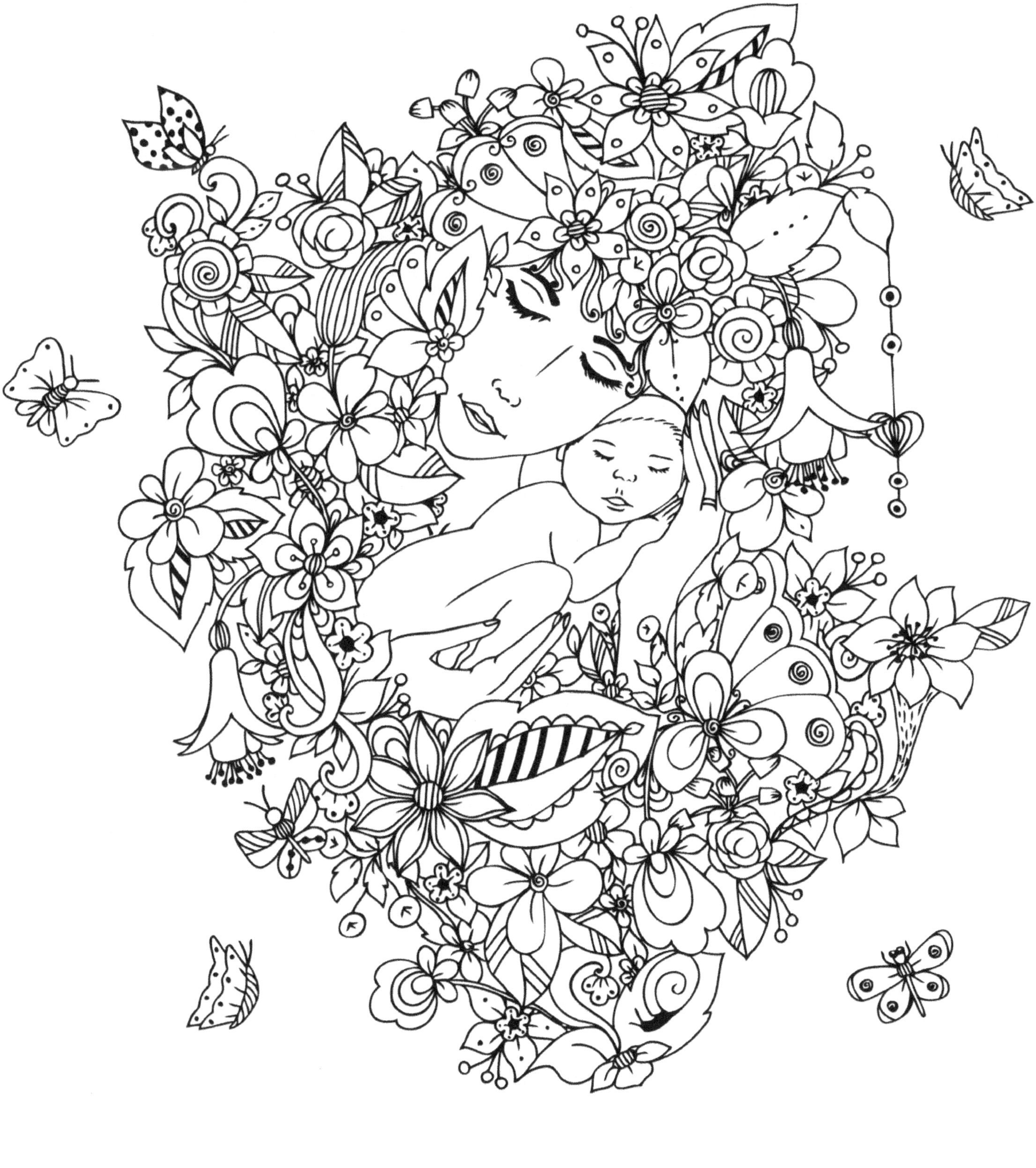

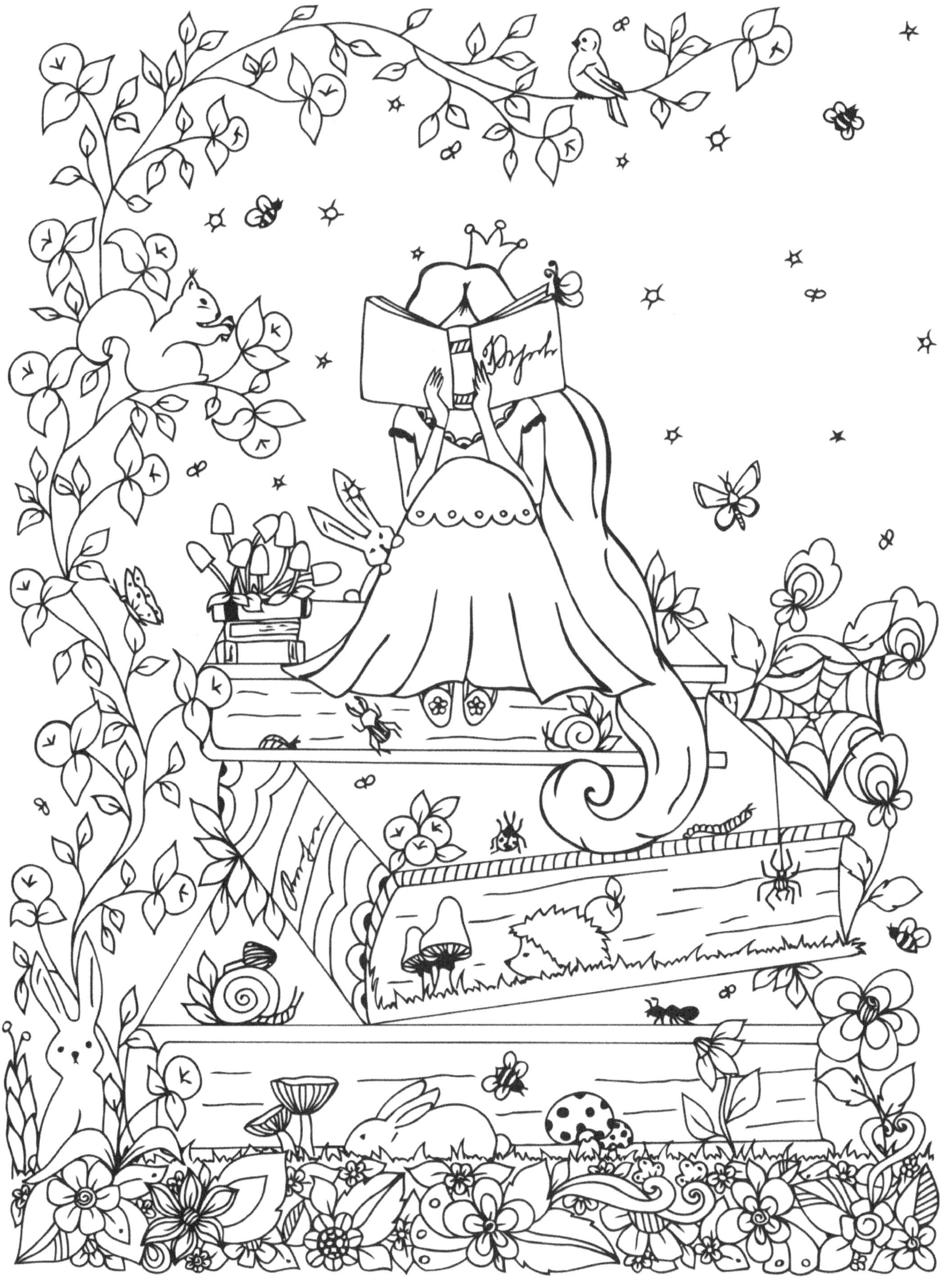

1.

Download Free 15 Coloring Pages
http://eepurl.com/cOjb1r

Made in the USA
Middletown, DE
25 March 2020